After my Friend was Murdered

By Christine Sanregret

After my Friend was Murdered

By Christine Sanregret

Cover by Selfpubbookcovers.com

Copyright 2018 Christine Sanregret

ISBN 978-1-989092-20-0

For privacy protection, some names have been changed.
Permission has been granted to use the stories and materials in the book.

Introduction

My name is Christine Sanregret and my Cree Native ancestors are from Batoche, Saskatchewan area. I grew up in Edmonton, Alberta with my sister, a Ukrainian Mother and a French Father hiding the Native part. My Grandfather was Cree and adopted into a Metis family at six years old to keep him safe from residential school.

His Native family would visit him, and he knew he was loved. In order to hide, my Grandfather took on his adoptive family name. My name is from my Grandfather's adoptive family and his real name is unknown along with what Native band he came from.

My children and I should have Native status, know what band our ancestors are from and have our ancestors name, but it is lost. I am grateful my Grandfather was kept safe from residential school even though the consequence amounted to losing our heritage. Later on after leaving home my sister and I got in touch with our Native background learning from many wonderful Native people from different tribal areas around Canada. This book is a collection of Spiritual experiences and healing teachings from Native people across Canada. For protection of privacy a few names have been changed.

Spiritual Background

My mother had premonitions of where she would feel things before they happened. My sister is an Astrologer and taught Palmistry. Spiritual experiences were normal to me being brought up with acceptance of these gifts. My sister and I receive messages from spirit when the messages are given. We are not able to call for messages from spirit like mediums but are able to receive messages periodically. My sister receives messages from spirit easier and more frequently than I do and is also contacted by spirit to pass messages on to me. I am very thankful to have many spiritual experiences and messages given to me to help me heal.

Purpose

My work as a Resident Care Aide in a twenty-four-hour care facility and most recent as a Community Health Worker has allowed me to assist those that are dying, needing to talk about death and their losses of loved ones. There are so many people in my travels in my daily life who want me to share my Spiritual experiences and Native teachings. What has benefited me is what I share with others to promote healing throughout my whole life whenever possible.

My experience has made me unafraid of death and I know I would not be doing such fulfilling work on this planet earth without the hardship of losing my friend and daughter. I will continue to share and assist others until it is time for me to cross over into the heavens. My intention is to help everyone feel more positive for our loved ones in spirit who have gone on ahead of us so we can live our lives happier on earth until we meet again. Let the amazement begin…

After My Friend Was Murdered

It was 1976 and my friend Melody and I has just graduated from High School. I was going to travel across Canada for a few months, then come back and move in with Melody. Melody was planning to move from her parent's farm to an apartment near the college where she was enrolled in the Criminology program.

On the Saturday night of the long weekend in August, Melody, a friend visiting from out of town, and I went to an all-night drive-in theatre. At 7am after the drive-in theatre we went for coffee and talked and laughed for a few hours and then Melody and her friend dropped me off at home.

That Sunday morning was the last time I saw Melody. Sunday evening Melody was taken from her car a quarter of a mile from home, murdered and dropped in a ditch twenty minutes away.

I was shattered and not a day went by without feeling deep inner sorrow. I appeared okay on the outside but really was devastated. I did not want to talk about it, feeling no one understood how I felt. I was mainly afraid of talking and opening up a flood of feelings that would break open a dam and never stop.

This world was awful and full of murderers and I lived in fear the murderers were out to get me next. How could something so awful happen to such a wonderful person? I worried how Melody was and agonized over the pain she must of suffered.

Visit To An Old Wise Woman Medium

At the age of twenty-two years, four years after Melody was

After my Friend was Murdered

murdered, I went to an old wise woman medium. As soon as I sat down in the office in her house, she said

"You lost someone who died at a young age and she has long dark hair, brown pants and a white top. She wants you to know she is happy in paradise somewhere like Hawaii, was bonked on the head and did not feel any pain, went out at that time. It was meant to be, had done something in another time, not this time, so had to go that way. It is not important for you to know what was done and it will not happen to you."

After seeing the wonderful old wise woman medium I had an understanding that helped me let go of so much sorrow, fear, anger and confusion. I felt like I had a ton of weight lifted off my shoulders. I knew there was more to this life involving other life times and now it made sense. This was a spiritual awakening and the beginning of much more to come.

Spiritual Experiences

The Hooded Rider

In the middle of the night I sat up in bed and watched a hooded rider on a tan colored horse gallop towards me and continue off to my left side. At that point I was afraid of seeing this vision from spirit even though it felt exciting at the same time. I knew that help was needed for me to learn what to do with seeing messages from spirit. I needed to learn how to stay with the light and positive spiritual realm.

Meditation

Started going to a meditation group which taught me to pray and ask for protection so only the highest, truest and the best be allowed to draw near. White light is also what I put around myself and this helps calm me down turning fear into faith. Seeing visions and having messages brought to me is a gift and I learned to keep my light shining. This way there is no room for negative to come around me. I have been blessed to learn some of my Native culture that I was not brought up with. Smudging is part of my Native culture that I have learned to practice with prayer whenever I need to bring in positive energy and clear negative energy or to center myself.

Rainbow Healing

After waking I was about to get up out of bed and was taken to the spirit world to a place and shown many important things including my purpose in this life. There was a large high ceiling room with a lot of different people.

Some people were dressed odd or had eccentric hair, jewelry and costumes. There were gypsies, priests, and many eccentric people standing out in the crowd of people.

Mixed in the crowd were people like me dressed and appeared relatively normal. It was understood by me that there was a rainbow of healing coming from the heavens above through me and flowing out of my heart area. This rainbow of healing from above is also sent to others with prayer by my mind to bring healing and love.

I have been sending this healing rainbow to others for years always with the intention to heal. A lot of these people could do the same as me with their minds with the rainbow healing. Most of the people promoted that the power was coming from them but clearly it comes from the heavens above not the person. I was told those who claim it is their power are not bad people as they just do not know.

All that matters is that they are giving energy to others and not taking. Taking energy from others is a sin. I went and sat by my friend's Mom who I have never met but knew she passed away. She held my hand and asked me to pray for her Native community as they are going through a hard time.

A lady came and gave me her baby to hold. As I was holding the baby, I brought the healing rainbow from above me flowing through me and the baby with my mind. The baby loved the healing energy and knew it was needed. The baby's Mom took the baby and these two men came to talk to me. The first man came and hugged me and said "you are amazing, you are an inconspicuous healer". This man's wife was standing at a distance smiling and so glad he was talking to me.

The next man who I thought was married also hugged me and whispered in my ear "I am not married." then took me to sit beside him on a bench. He expressed how glad he was to finally find me and was not going anywhere away from me. I knew he was doing the same work on this planet as me and understood without words.

As I was floating back into my body, I was thinking this is the kind of partner I need. Someone who understands our work on this planet earth where we go do what we need to do then come together when we can. In a space where there are no games and everything is understood.

When I came back into my body I thought of this man and recalled how his head looked from behind, but I could not remember his face. Since this wonderful experience I understand my purpose of inconspicuous healing and now consciously practice it every day. I pray, ask for heavenly help and send the rainbow as an easy visual in my mind to certain people and the whole world. The rainbow relates to the chakra energy points and healing the of our mind, body and spirit.

Christine Sanregret

Melody's Visit

My friend Melody who is in spirit came to visit me while I was driving my car by myself. I was changing the channels on the radio trying to find something to listen to and Melody said in my ear to keep the song on the radio. The song was a Neil Sedaka song and I knew immediately it was Melody as she loved Neil Sedaka. I thought Neil Sedaka's music was not the coolest music especially when we were in High School and found it amusing and cute that Melody liked this. So I kept the entire song on and listened to it with so much love as I felt my friend in spirit there with me.

Week Before Labour

A week before I was going to have my second baby, I was very nervous and emotional. My sister had Melody come to her in spirit and tell her that she is so close to me that if I am by myself and see someone trip and if I laugh she will be laughing with me. She also is so close to me that she feels my tears. She said there is a lot of love around me and to stop feeling sorry for myself.

Well I stopped immediately feeling sorry for myself especially since I did not need to have Melody in spirit feel my tears anymore. From that day on my attitude changed to realizing the good around me instead of my self pity - Boo Hoo Wah Wah Wah.

My Embarrassing Trip

Melody came in spirit to my sister to tell her a message only Melody and I knew about. It was a day in High School Melody and I were walking across the street to go for coffee. A green car stopped and she said you had your long hair, white sweater and high heeled clogs and tripped while walking in front of the green car.

In the green car was my ex-boyfriend that I laughed at for frequently tripping while walking. Oh My Gawd that was not the person I wanted to walk in front of stumbling across the street while he watched. Melody said she laughed so hard she almost pissed her pants. Melody added she appreciated and loved how we were always laughing at everything and anything we could. Finding humour in everyday things is what I continue to do wherever possible and I am very fortunate my sister Judy is right there with me. We might not see each other every day but we manage to talk and laugh on the phone a few times a week.

Daughter's High School Production

My daughter was in a High School production helping to correograph, preform a solo and do some of the group singing and dancing acts. When the show was about to start I was sitting in the front row end seat beside the cameraman. I was feeling nervous and anxious but also sad because my sister was not able to be there.

I was starting to cry and felt a hand on my shoulder and heard Melody in spirit say "it's okay I am here." There was no one beside me on that side and the cameraman was behind his camera. I stopped crying and then was filled with exhilaration knowing that Melody was there watching the show with me. Wow what a night!

Relationship Breakup

Was having difficulty in going through a break up and was shown in a dream message where my man and I were walking side by side down a path in harmony. The path led to a vee separating into two paths. One to the left showed it was running your own life path. The other to the right was following God's will. I was going to the right following God's will and it was easy for me. The words to the song "I know where I am going, do you want to come too" by the Judds was what was on my mind as I walked.

Understanding came that I know where I am going and the man I was with was welcome to come walk with me. If not I will keep going alone as I know where I need to keep walking. The man I was with had one foot on the left path. I was then told by spirit that "you have come as far as you can go with this soul, this soul has a choice to make".

Well this man made the choice to go on the path to the left and tried to get me to go with him. I knew what the path on the left was like as I was following it in the past and there was no way I was going back there. I easily kept walking to the right and felt he was welcome to walk beside me if he chose to.

In my life this is what has happened many times. Since this message was given to me I understand it simply and give my best with each relationship experience not knowing until I reach the vee of both paths that it is the end with each man. The only thing I feel is walking side by side in harmony then as we reach the vee there is a shift. The shift feels very uncomfortable with the harmony gone. It is then I keep walking happily on my own.

Standing On A Beach

Going through all the feelings in relationships is not as easy as it sounds to me. I still get scared of the feelings and emotionally feel I am going to drown. I was shown a dream message to help me deal with a new relationship.

As I am standing on a beach when I meet a soul, I need to experience a relationship with, it shows that I need to get in the water one step at a time. I do not need to dive in the deep end and feel like drowning. I just need to slide in slowly and test the waters one step at a time and remind myself I can always get out if I need to.

This calms me and helps me get over anxious and scary feelings. I also remind myself it is good to be a little scared and feel more alive. So I pick up my guts and go one step at a time.

Christine Sanregret

Walking My Dad

My Dad was in the Veteran's Hospital for the last part of his life. One morning I was awake laying in my bed ready to get up. Before I could get up out of bed, I was taken on a spiritual journey where I met my Dad at a tunnel. I walked him halfway through the tunnel and saw my Grampa, Gramma and Great Uncle at the end. They had green grass and bright sunshine behind them and I could feel their love as they waved for my Dad to come with them.

I pointed to them and said, "See Dad they are waiting for you, you can go now, it's okay". Then as I was coming back to my body I could feel what it was like when my Dad used to carry me in his arms when I was a baby. Ahh I loved that feeling… next I was back in my body and got up to tell my Mom and my sister that I just walked Dad halfway through the tunnel. We talked about how my Dad will cross over into the heaven's soon. Well it took 2 1/2 years for my Dad to go but I am glad I was able to help in some way to make it easier.

Daughter's Passing

My younger daughter Jaymie was in a car accident at the age of twenty-three years. Even though it was absolutely devastating, she made it easier to accept by letting me and others know she is still around. Her spirit came to my sister while we were talking so she could give me the message she was hit on the head and went out of her body at that time. Two angels came and got her and there was no confusion and did not feel any pain. The autopsy confirmed she had a head injury.

After my Friend was Murdered

Occurrences A Few Weeks Before Jaymie's Passing

Co-worker's Feelings Of Dying In A Car Accident

A co-worker of mine had just come back from days off saying he felt like he was going to get in a car and die in an accident. He said it wasn't going to happen to him and that he felt it was going to happen to someone else. He said he felt like the person who was going to pass away in the accident was at peace with it. My Daughter passed away a few weeks later in a car accident.

Christine Sanregret

While Working Nights At A Twenty Four Hour Care Facility

A resident where I worked came from her room at the end of the hall in the middle of the night to get me to come to her room to see this angel man across the street floating above the trees. This resident never did this in the middle of the night. I went to her room and saw an angel man floating above the trees across the street with his hands outstretched by his sides. My coworker came to look and he could not see the angel man but he said someone is going to pass soon. My Daughter passed away a few weeks later and this resident passed away a few months later.

Picture Of Angel Man In The Sky

I went to visit my friend at a coffee shop and this lady with downs syndrome came over to me and gave me this picture of an angel man in the sky. When this lady gave me the picture she had such loving eyes and said "I want you to have this". This picture was an angel man formed by clouds with his hands outstretched and down by his sides just like I saw in the resident's room across the street floating above the trees. Jaymie passed away a few weeks later. Jaymie in spirit gave a message to my sister to give to me that two angels came and got her when she had her car accident.

After my Friend was Murdered

Christine Sanregret

Occurrences After Jaymie's Passing

Song For Celebration Of Life

Jaymie came in spirit to my sister to tell her she wanted Michelle her older sister to sing "Love Can Build A Bridge" at her celebration of life. Michelle was ten years old in a talent show at school and did not know how to work the microphone, so she sang one part really loud.

Her classmates teased her so that song she avoided singing in public but would sing it for Jaymie privately whenever she asked. Right after I hung up the phone, Michelle phoned me and said she knows what song she is going to sing. Jaymie in spirit also gave Michelle the message she wanted that song. Michelle was given the chance to record the song on disc by a talented friend of Jaymie's and it could not have turned out better.

You Just Don't Have Your Tickets Yet

Jaymie came in spirit to me since she knew I was having difficulty wondering how I was going to handle letting my Mom go when she passes. I did not anyone else around me to pass away, it hurts too much.

Jaymie's message was: "Mom just think of it like I went on a trip to paradise and I am waiting for you. Grammy is coming to meet me sooner than you. You just don't have your tickets yet". This is how I look at people passing around me and whenever possible I carry Jaymie's message to others.

Four Months After Jaymie Passed Away

Jaymie in spirit gave me and my sister a message that she did not nod off to sleep and vere off the road, then over correct her steering sending her tumbling down the road and landing upside down back on the Cocahailla highway. She was reading a text message while driving and it only looked like falling asleep at the wheel.

Facebook Page

About four months after Jaymie passed away her facebook page showed a thumbs up that she liked a link that can be downloaded to have text messages verbally communicated while driving for safety. This was on Jaymie's facebook page for a few weeks and some of her friends saw it also. At first they thought who has her password but then realized it was Jaymie from heaven trying to help others to safely have texts communicated verbally instead of reading texts while driving.

Jaymie's Boo

One morning I had the day off and was sleeping away, then I heard Jaymie in spirit beside my bed say "Boo" at 7am. I could feel her laughing just like she always did as I was scared out of my tree.

Jaymie Singing

I worked nightshifts starting at 11pm until 7am at a Long Term Care

Facility as a Resident Care Aide. I was laying in bed awake before getting up to get ready for my shift and suddenly I was taken out of my body to the spirit world. I was in the first row and up on stage was Jaymie in a lilac dress with a white collar and cuffs on three quarter sleeves.

She sang a beautiful song with a soulful voice I had imagined she could if she would have continued on training her voice with singing lessons. Jaymie wanted to sing like her sister Michelle but did not have the patience to train her voice. As it was Jaymie took one singing lesson and then was on to other things.

She would sing in her room really loud out of tune and burst into song often torturing us with this awful voice. Meanwhile Jaymie thought she sang well and nooobody could tell her she was a horrible singer. Now here I was watching Jaymie on stage singing in a beautiful soulful voice. She brought me over in the spirit world to show me that she worked on her patience training her voice which was something she had wanted to accomplish while she was here on earth.

While I was traveling in the spirit world to go back in my body, I thought Jaymie looks so beautiful. I did not think she could be more beautiful than she was on earth two years before but now she was even more radiantly beautiful in the spirit world. I was back in my body needing to quickly get ready for work. I felt like I was jumping for joy with what I had just experienced and had no time to call anyone. It was all I could do to go to work feeling on top of the world with no one to tell. I had to wait until I got off work in the morning to phone my sister. Wow thank you, thank you, thank you!

Christine Sanregret

Healing Journey

The next part of this book is a collection of some Native Medicine Wheel teachings and healing exercises. When on my learning path of my Native background I was given teachings from Native people across Canada. They want their Native teachings to be shared with everyone, not just Native people so it can be passed on. The Medicine Wheel is used by Native people for teaching balance. The format is a circle divided by four equal parts. Most Native teachings were given to me as a story or an experiential activity which is how they are shared in this book.

Living In Harmony

The first Medicine Wheel is Living In Harmony by Chief Albert Lightning from Hobema Alberta. This teaching was drawn on a flip chart simply by a Native elder while sharing to the group of people at the Elders Symposium. We drew along with the Native elder on our own sheet of paper.

Start with drawing a large circle divided into four quarters. Draw a few trees in left top quarter and write

Honesty. Draw a braid of sweetgrass in bottom left quarter and write **Gentleness**. Draw a few mountains in top right quarter and write **Respect**. Draw a few horses in bottom right quarter and write **Sharing**.

The example given is my simple drawing of the Medicine Wheel teaching of Living In Harmony and may be copied to create your own on your choice of paper.

After my Friend was Murdered

Christine Sanregret

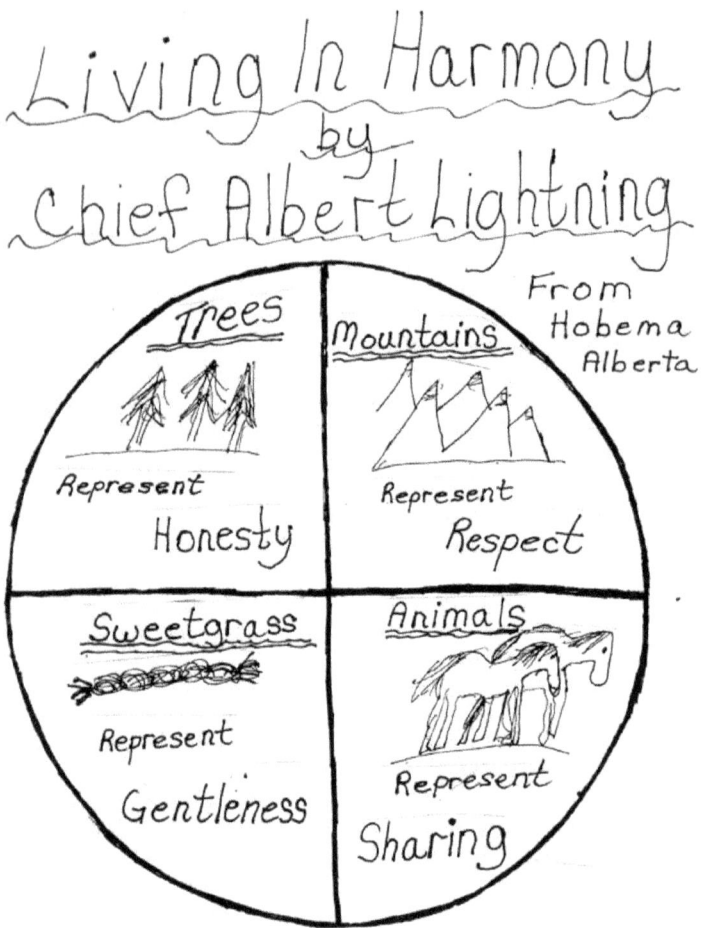

Chief Albert Lightning teaches if each of us are responsible to learn and practice Honesty, Gentleness, Respect and Sharing we can live in Harmony.

Keep Your Light Shining Bright

Wendy a Native counsellor from Manitoba shared how she has many people brought to her who have never looked inside. She says to them they need to be willing to go to the root if she is able to help them. Most agree to go to the root for the counselling treatment. Wendy says she sees a column of light in the middle of our body and the light is the love we have for ourselves. The column of light gets filled with garbage all the way from childhood.

Wendy says she uses timeline therapy for going back to childhood to present. She begins with a Native Smudge praying for the Creator, the Ancestors and Loved Ones in spirit to come and help with whatever needs to brought out for healing. Wendy said they cry like babies as this is needed to clean the garbage out so our light can shine bright.

Self Care Plan

The second Medicine Wheel teaching purpose is to bring balance with taking care of yourself.

In the first quarter write a minimum of four ways for your physical care.

Write a minimum of four ways for your mental care in the second quarter.

In the third quarter write a minimum of four ways for your emotional care.

Write a minimum of four ways for your spiritual care in the fourth quarter.

An example of a Self Care Plan with some suggestions is provided. A blank Self Care Plan is provided for your own use which may be copied and filled out. Make extra copies for additions and revisions to your own self care plan.

As time goes on you may find new ways to create balance with taking care of yourself which makes filling in a new self care plan easy with extra copies.

Healthy Ways To Express Anger

It is okay to be mad, it is not okay to be mean. The following list of healthy ways to express anger gives ideas to use to create an easier and happier way to live.

Keep cleaning out the garbage so your light can shine bright.

The list is given with room for additional ideas to be added.

* Go for a walk

* Talk to someone

* Cry

* Go to a quiet place for alone time

* Meditate

* Pray

* Listen to music

* Beat on a drum

* Run

* Swim

* Dance

* Go to the Gym

* Rake leaves or shovel snow

* Throw rocks into a pond

After my Friend was Murdered

* Ask for a hug

* Write

* Take deep breaths

* _____

* _____

* _____

* _____

* _____

* _____

* _____

Christine Sanregret

SELF CARE PLAN

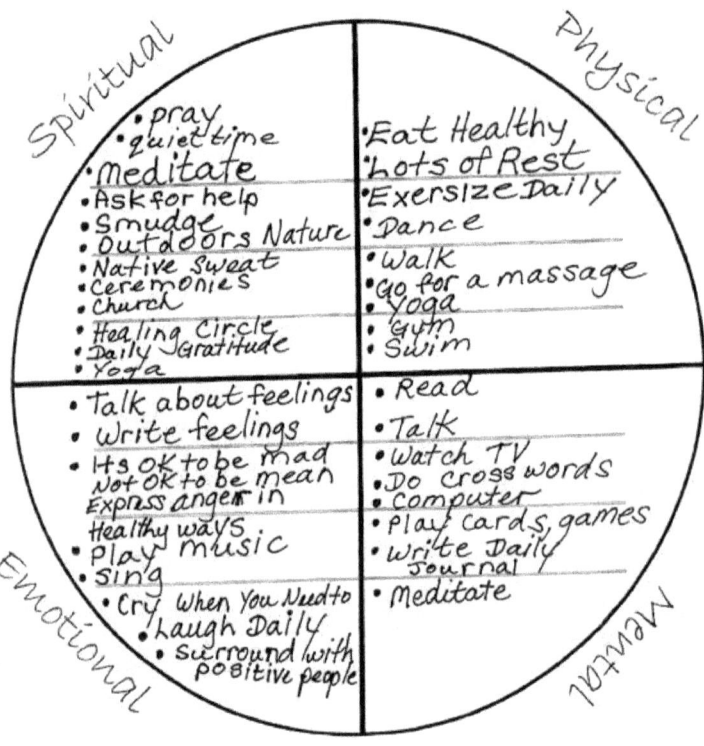

Example

After my Friend was Murdered

SELF CARE PLAN

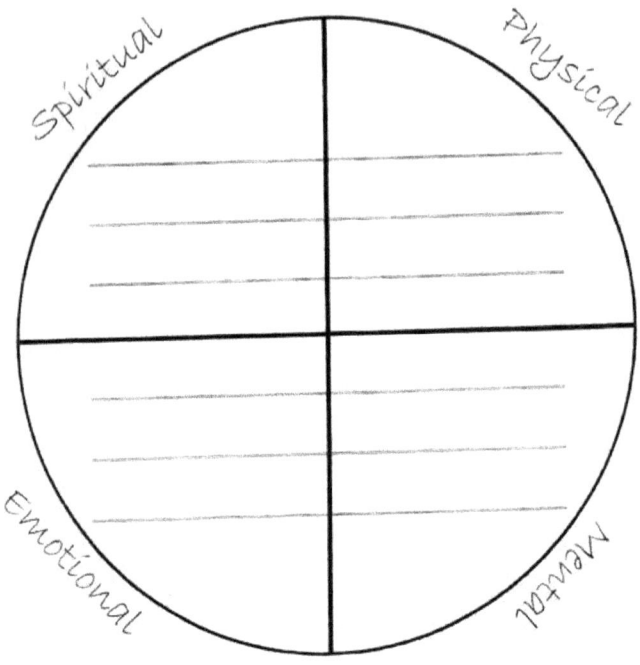

Circle of Life

The third Medicine Wheel teaching for Circle of Life starts with a circle divided by four quarters. The purpose of this Medicine Wheel teaching Circle of Life is to build self esteem and to celebrate your life.

The first top right quarter is from age one to twenty-five.

Second bottom right quarter is from age twenty-six to fifty.

Third bottom left quarter is from age fifty-one to seventy-five.

Last top left quarter is from seventy-six to one hundred years old.

Start by drawing lines and writing accomplishments all the way to your present age. Accomplishments can be learning to ride a bike, becoming a parent or whatever you want as long as it is an accomplishment.

When you look at your last accomplishment up to your present age you will notice the rest of the circle has blank space left. The space that is left on your Circle of Life is for you to add more of your accomplishments in the future.

Look forward to how are you going to fill your space for the rest of your life. Honour yourself for all your accomplishments so far in your life. An example of a Circle of Life Medicine Wheel teaching suggestions and a blank Circle of Life are provided.

The blank Circle of Life page may be copied and filled out or drawn on a flip chart sheet.

Christine Sanregret

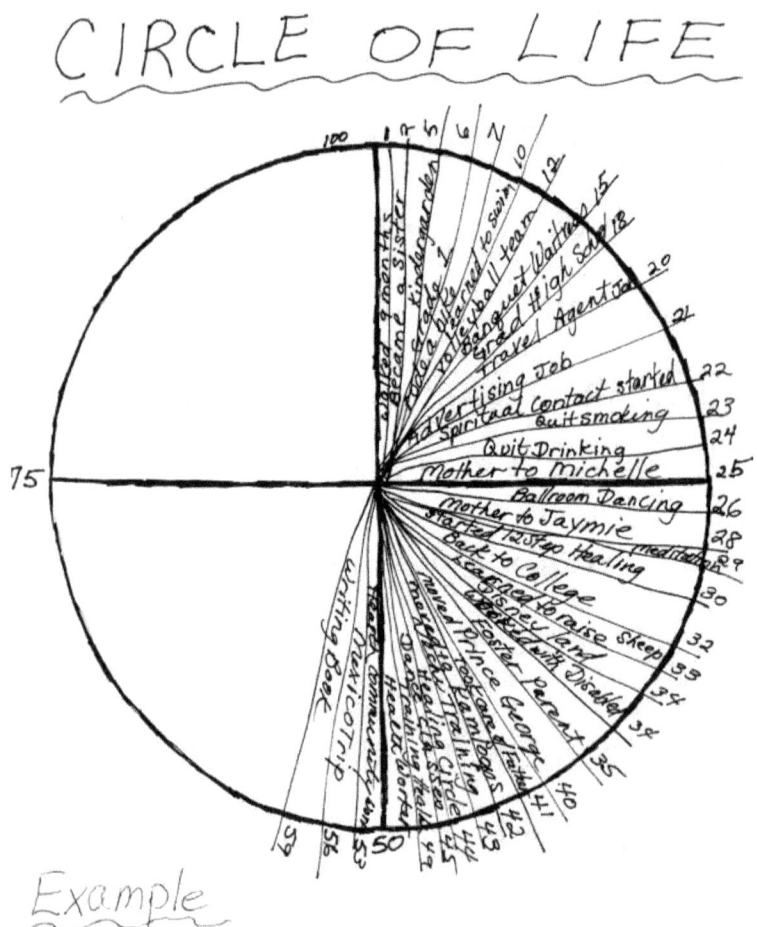

Example

After my Friend was Murdered

Christine Sanregret

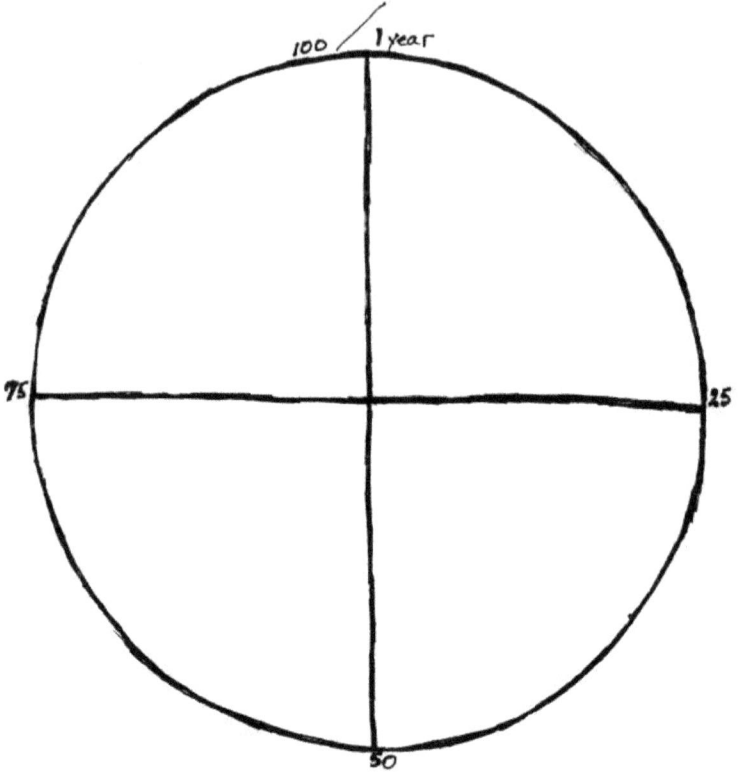

Acknowledgements

Poundmakers Round Dance, St. Albert AB

Enoch Sweat Ceremony With Raven And Rita Mackinaw, Enoch AB

Yuwipi Ceremony, Lethbridge AB

Elders Symposium, Edmonton AB

Aboriginal Planning & Training With Rita Matthew, Kamloops BC

Native Healing Circles With Jean Stenhouse, Kamloops BC

Healing Circle With Fire Keepers, Peniwa MB

Flying On Your Own With Aboriginal Employment Centre, Kamloops BC

True Colors Training, Kamloops BC

Nechi Community Addictions Training, Chase BC

Sundance Ceremony, Chase BC

Ghost Dance Ceremony, Chase BC

Batoche National Historical Site, Batoche SK

Yuwipi Ceremony, Kamloops BC

Share Your Spiritual Experiences

If you have any stories of your own about spiritual happenings which showed you the way or offered healing I would love to read them and perhaps share them on my blog or in a second book.

Send to christinewithoutregret@gmail.com

Any stories submitted may be combined and shared in a book or blog page with names changed for protection of privacy. Unless you state you do not wish your story used in this way, sharing your story will be taken as permission.

Celticfrog Publishing is a small independent press which works with selected clients to get their book out in the world.

After my Friend was Murdered